Thus Spake Gigolo

Thus Spake Gigolo

by Scott Bailey

NYQ Books™

The New York Quarterly Foundation, Inc.
New York, New York

NYQ Books™ is an imprint of The New York Quarterly Foundation, Inc.

The New York Quarterly Foundation, Inc.
P. O. Box 2015
Old Chelsea Station
New York, NY 10113

www.nyq.org

First Edition

Set in New Baskerville

Layout by Kimberly Boland

Library of Congress Control Number: 2014945818

ISBN: 978-1-63045-002-1

Thus Spake Gigolo

Acknowledgements

Grateful acknowledgment to the editors of the following magazines in which these poems first appeared, ALL in previous versions:

The Adirondack Review, "Bildungsroman," and "Convergence" previously titled "Backwards Pedaling."

Exquisite Corpse, "Greyhound," "Probation," "Jail," "Bond," "Court," "Death," "Gigolo," "Do I Dare Disturb the Universe?" "Aunt Louise and Space Shuttle Challenger," and "Polaroid Funeral" previously titled "Picture Frames and Uncle James."

Harpur Palate, "Why I Should Stand for Jesus?"

The Journal, "Grits Saved Me."

Meridian, "Birth."

New York Quarterly, "Exit Ramp 69 in Eatonville, Mississippi," "Hallows," and "Sugar Hill."

Psychology Tomorrow Magazine, "On the Other Side."

Rofous City Review, "Goodwill."

Southern Quarterly, "Pasture."

The Cortland Review, "The Lost Supper" previously titled "The Last Supper."

The Southeast Review, "The Aristocracy of the Plow," and "Fire."

Verse Daily, "Fire."

Contents

1

Dedicated to Ken Watson

1

Grits Saved Me

If it weren't for grits, I wouldn't have lived.

Before I was born, a preacher prophesied, his hand holding my mom's
And said I was a special child and a devil wanting to kill me.

And sure enough, my head was so big, Mom, risking the wrath of Dad,
Had two male nurses on top of her, pushing me out.

And since then, the devil's been after my life all my life,
But luckily I spoke in tongues, my aunt leading me to Jesus

On the women's side of the altar, making me ready for that devil
                Crouching, grinning and leering

Beside my bed, eyes and teeth
Volcano red, ready to burn what wasn't his.

But as soon as Mom turned the light on,
Her face warm as a wash cloth, loving as a page of St. Matthew,

I asked her for a bowl of grits—a bowl of grits with butter—
And I held those grits, like my tongue holding on to God.

Fire

We burn the fields, and it seems the whole world's on fire,
As if the seventh seal opens to a silence in heaven.

I'm told to watch for flames that jump the guided path
And to be weary of the heads of horses that will be as the heads of lions,

Learning how to burn, so the grass returns like the blunted tail of a lizard,
The herb yielding seed after seed, the corn, so pure, weevils crowd its teeth,

And watermelons when thumped echo the Holy Ghost.
        This time, lost with the thought of worshipping the beast,

His head on my hips, gently turning me over,
I forget myself.

The fire gets out, blackens the siding of our house.
I hose what I can, but fire's a beheaded chicken, not knowing where to go, just going.

Birth

In the air, honeysuckles and a polecat, rife and wild,
        I witness a birth: A cow's belly swollen solid, A calf's legs half out.

        Sliced open, her calf flops out with a membrane,
    A cord strangling the neck.

    I watch their legs chained to a tractor
        And dragged to trees scratched by antlers, left with velvet.

            Atop and between those trees where they rotted,
        I lie on a hammock
    Of vines that loosen, lowering me to their bones:

            Her face with briars,
        Her calf with fungi.

Nearby, a pond with algae so thick, how do fish breathe?
        And on that bank, crows gorge on a moccasin.

    I walk knowing what many already know—

The body betrays us all.

Aristocracy of the Plow

1.

We scale the fish, nail their heads to the barn,
               The grass glimmering with pearl-like shavings.

2.

We walk the field where he speaks of the sycamore the tax collector climbs,
         The dogwood a remembrance of our sins.

3.

Under a yellow plum tree, we eat baloney-mayonnaise sandwiches
        Before cane-poling the highest plums down,
              Then we head back to check the trap for owls.

4.

Speaking in tongues, he baptizes me, us all, in his catfish pond.
        We drain that pond every year, eating fish eggs for weeks.

5.

He visions a revival: cars for miles, parked on the roadside, in both directions:
>   Women slinging hairpins from beehive hairdos,
>   Men running around the pews, their key chains like tambourines.

6.

Grandma wails over the casket, which I help carry, a pocket bible under his armpit,
>   Psalms 1:3 stuffed in his lapel:
>   He is like a tree planted by streams of water.

7.

On a white stretcher rolling down a pebble-cement step,
>   He grabs my hand when a wheel catches a door's hinge,
>   "Pray while tending to the cows."

Harvest Moon

In the woods, I barely dodge an equally terrified pine
In awe of my brother Randy dousing gasoline on our trash-pile fire,
A backyard-sore, not the fire, the dump that won't ever burn,
Or burn out, so I uncoil the water hose from our vinyl/tar-paper home.
Randy wrestles me down, pins my head to the ground, shoves dirt
In my mouth, makes me watch the fire closing in, burning
Into a black-eye pea around our propane tank. I piss my pants,
Shit my britches, so Randy lets me up, shoots at me, misses, misses twice—
Bullets like yellow jackets stinging dirt—
                    So he puts the pistol
To his head, he pulls the trigger, but, but the chamber jams.
This night, I pray for tongues, on the women's side
Of the altar. I feel like fire ants all over, like a wet towel wrung dry
Between worlds, between dreams, in the order I've been received.
I throw up on Sister Lowry, I run out to the parking lot
And ask the Lord, How about taking me now,
Save me the trouble of climbing the circus-tent pole to the top,
Before I peek out its navel, before I self-explode?
                    A harvest moon crowns
The hill behind our church, a hazard light
Around a pot-hole, a yolk on steroids, a cytoplasm-cherry, a core,
A nucleus, a neutron, a fucking-scary situation, so near, the world
May surely burn, the end at hand, all because Randy's out

Of hand, and I want it so. I'd rather learn to say Amen

To the error of my family's ways, my ways,

      To love to hate the I,

            To favor the convincing, blurring lie.

Pasture

I walk a pasture the day Dad quits sweet tea for Jesus.

    Beagles chase the scent of rabbits or squirrels,

        And the sky's one cloud of tractor tracks.

           "Give up sumpin'," I hear him say, "To make heaven your home."

              The sun a beam of light through oak trees,

                 A ray on a barn's sagging, rusty-tin roof

                    Overgrown with honeysuckles seeping through holes.

                Wisteria wraps a car that he and Mom honeymooned in,

            Its rear-view mirror gone, ants routing a muffler,

        A rose bush growing through its floorboard,

    Not quitting until it reaches the steering wheel, craning out the window.

"Gotta suffer," I hear him say, "Heaven ain't for free, my son."

    Cousins play Red Rover between cornrows,

        Water bugs gather like beads on twigs

           Sheltering them from the throats of fish.

              There's no giving up for me, I give him that.

              Enough has been taken,

                And now he wants sweet tea, forget that.

              I give up my youth.

                I must give that away.

Convergence

I'm thirteen and allergic to cockroach saliva when Dad buys me a Huffy
With a digital speedometer.

From then on, life explodes, like drinking a hormone Molotov cocktail—
Peach fuzz,   crop-eared haircut,   pencil mustache—

    At the top of a hill,
        We hold hands, legs lifting above spinning pedals at an unregistered speed,

The coasting too fast, I let go.

Sex will be different for me than for him:
A backward,   brakeless   pedaling.

Why Should I Stand for Jesus?

When I win four hundred dollars at the National Tobacco Spitting Contest,
I buy a Civic, the paint peeling. I feel a Holy-Ghost freedom when I pass
The fat, grinning, rich, daddy's boy who calls me Buckteeth Ugly, laughing
At my fake Reeboks. When he passes me in his silver Trans Am,

Bumper sticker Eat My Grits, I floor it; my motor blows, and I coast
To the side of the road, fat boy flipping me the bird, driving on,
Most likely to Wards for a Big One. I walk down a hill to a porch
Where an old woman stitches a quilt; she tells me to take it slow,

Just as she is, sipping on a glass of warm milk, sitting in her rocker,
Waiting for her dogs, already in heaven, who met their fates
On the road. I call Dad on her phone, a red rotary box, just like Grandma's
On the wall, under a stuffed sea bass that Grandpa caught while

Honeymooning on the coast. Dad arrives, tractor chain in hand,
And I drive attached to his beat-up blue Chevrolet with dents from pulp-wooding,
The truck that my cousin and I drive to downtown Magee.
It's Crazy Day, an annual event—wooden ducks, benches with heart-shaped backs,

Peanut brittle, hotdogs and powdered doughnuts—that kind of crazy;
People crowd the streets to show off fancy cars, sparkling rims, spoilers,
Motorola antennas. We never score a date, only invitations for mud-bog,
Beer-guzzles. After months of looking, we place a newer-model motor

In an older-junk frame. Dad loans it to me after my brother wrecks his car,
Missing a woman in her elderly scooter, but hitting a hamburger shack.
The body's not completely totaled, so Uncle Ulmer and Dad
Repeatedly pull the car with a tractor into a pine until it's beyond repair.

When we realize that the pine won't live, the sapling my brother
Won as a prize for selling the most pies for Smokey-the-Bear Awareness Week,
It's a cold morning before school, the day my classmates swear to a walkout
When our teachers don't get a raise. I crank the car, such God-awful screaming.

I pop the hood to find guts, stool, hair, and fluffy tail pieces splattered
All over that newly installed motor. Another kitten, its butt bald without a tail,
Wobbles out from under the car that dies and won't crank, so I have to ride
The bus, bus 125 where I fight Tanya. Four years prior, she slaps my glasses

Off, calls me Sissy. I slam her on the floorboard and commence to punch,
Then her tall brother's on my back, scratching me, kids screaming, Kick that bitch's ass!
Till this day, I don't know if they were referring to me or to Tanya.
Her father comes to our house, and Dad whips me with a switch,

Tells her father that I won't cause any more trouble. I'm confused.
I'm just standing up for myself. But Dad says if I'm doing any standing up,
I should be standing for Jeeeazuss. He drives a forklift at a plant all day,
So he knows the importance of standing. The walkout is a success,

Because we make it on T.V. despite Principal Bowen demanding that we return
To class, but we say, Hell No! We Won't Go, all the way down Main Street.
I hear that Tanya has a lazy eye with stigmatism, like a team of horses
Pulling in opposing directions. She's married, wearing Dollar General

Makeup and feeding her kids bologna and welfare-cheese sandwiches.
That serves her right. Maybe, she'll think twice before slapping another sissy.
Who knows where she and Fat Boy end, but I know Uncle Ulmer's
Tilling gardens and Grandpa's spilling heavenly seeds, that old lady

Taking it slow, stitching, sipping on a glass of milk, alongside her dogs
Panting with purring kittens, all watching Dad drive that forklift
While praying to win the lottery. I don't want to live or die. I want to be.

Public Revelation of Love is Deadly to Love, Most Instances

Valentines Day, 1990

One Sunday-morning service, a traveling minister
Delivers a sermon about a preacher and a deacon
Having homo sex in the fellowship hall,
& they got stuck together like two dogs in heat,
Had to be carried out on a single stretcher,
Before God, family, friends, even sinners,
& gossip descended upon them like buzzards.
No wonder, I'm traumatized by anticipation,
On the backseat of our Ford Fairlane,
My brother, beside me, quoting Leviticus,
"A man shall not lie with a man,
    A man shall not know another man,"
Mom yelling, "Don't cast your pearls before a swine, son,"
        So I roll the window down,
    I spit, I scream, I claim, "I'm no swine, I'm a swan."
Dad slams the brake on our muddy driveway,
& we crash-slide into the front porch.
    We enter the backdoor to bible drills,
        Walls with exposed wires that hiss, hiss, wires that writhe—
       —

    On this night,   I have a dream as troubled as my days:
I throw a book

        That boomerangs

Back,

    I jump on

        Only to

        Slip off

           Into a ditch

              Of gushing water

Bent on   drowning me.

I wake, kicking & screaming, like each morning, "God, you're a Bully."

—

Six years later, that minister is sentenced to prison
For screwing his paralyzed cousin in a convalescence home.

—

      I may be a

    Butt Pirate, a born-again Rump-Wrangler, a Hemorrhoid hit-man, an Anal Astronaut speaking in tongues,
But I'm not that special, not that desperate,
Yet.

Aunt Louise and Space Shuttle Challenger

No matter how much faith she has, she's afraid of strong wind.
If weather's fair, she rocks on her porch, sipping sweet tea.
"Old dreamer's drink," she says, "Spirit water,"

Where she visions a clock spinning on the nose of a shuttle
Rising like cornbread in a hot, iron skillet,
Smoke billowing to the ground where people stand in shock,

Their heads upward, she's there too,
Her hands shaking, her body electric, in church NOW
Where she prophesizes—a voice fancier than her own, "Time introduces us to dus'."

Polaroid Funeral

The more my family goes, I pose   with open caskets.

The Passing should be as the   Living,   not in frames—

Uncle James joins the mantle   on nails   bending out the wall.

I'm the scrawny boy on his knees,   looking away,

Counting the carnations,   hoping this isn't real,   this ain't really my life.

Down Exit Ramp 69 in Eatonville, Mississippi

In Memory of Kenneth Watson

On a riverbank of muddy water with a current able to swift us under,
        Unleash a longing, so deep and tired of sleeping,

He says, "That was my first blow-job from a guy."
    Sure. And ham hangs from a window of a home I don't own, curing.

On our way home,
I'm speeding, he's reading from a book as big as his lap,

    "I am He that Aches with Love."
I'm elsewhere, yet, there,

        Clear and sweet is all that is my soul,
        And clear and sweet is all that is not my soul,

My hands in Whitman's pants, mapping his back with a blade of grass.

    We have a blowout, speeding off an exit ramp through trees,
The grill grating the hill like a wedge of cheese,

The windows down, sunroof open, a lively, dead breeze.
Hallelujah to my downshifting, to someone other than myself, steering.

On the roadside, are we alive or dead?
We don't know as we watch a raccoon making his way to a nest,

A sparrow swooping, willing to give her life for her young.
A cardinal, a mocking bird and a speckled bird swoop, too.

The raccoon returns to the ground,
Empty-handed.

The Lost Supper

for Leilani Hall

I ask if she's eating and her answer is "Beans."

        "If anything breaks" she says, "It means to."

    This is her childhood tattoo:
    Hours full of shelling beans—

       Sorting the undeveloped from the developed

1

Walking on her father's back, before cancer

2

Hazy face in a hospital gown

3

Bald head in hospital air—a clean cold.

She says, "I'm ready to go."

    Delirium, I say, This too shall pass, as I carry her to the river.

Bailey leads the way, barking and chasing the shadow of his tail under the moon.

I undress her, easing her into the water,

Look how much disturbance you cause.

She doesn't know that she's as lovely as forms passing in skies.

I paraphrase Shelley: let's take a jet where butterflies dream.

Keats suggests that in order to achieve a soul one must suffer.

Then there's Buddha: the move from happiness and suffering is genuine bliss.

Sometimes, I, too, want to wake to sleep, or I'd rather not sleep at all.

On the Other Side

In Memory of Grandpa

All's in motion, as if under water, from the height of an oak
Crippled by wind, a sky of fibrous clouds too thin to cause shadows.

I float down arms bowed to the ground
Where he's among wild onions conquering a chicken roost:

He's skinning a squirrel, flinging squirrel guts to cats.
"What's waiting for me? What will undo me?" I ask.

He points to a hawk waiting for a chick to stray from its mother.
He says, "We all need somebody, but we can make it ourselves."

     I remember him placing my kittens in a bread bag,
Beating them against a birch tree, not out of pleasure,

Out of mercy—   worms in their necks, worms he called wolves,
    Worms eating their way out, as if coming up for air.

Life's too short, too long to live dismayed.

Sugar Hill

Bare ruined choirs where late the sweet birds sang
—Shakespeare

Goats move on,
    Their hooves clicking,
Their stinking breaths

No longer chomping grass
    Now replaced by gravel-pit dust
And lovers whose shadows are one.

Not one word spoken,
    Their lips touching, despite a rotting peach tree,
Limbs a murderous chorus of crows.

Hallows

1

I have to give out pocket-sized Bibles instead of candy.
I'm beat on the bus, and I can't trick-or-treat.
The church does arrange a yearly Hayride to Boykin Church
Known for lynchings during and after service at the end
Of a dirt road surrounded by owlish woods and oil pumps.
Our uncles hide behind trees and jump out when we pass them.

2

I pass out when I see my brother holding my cat's head down,
Beating her tail with a ball-peen hammer. My parents call him
A mean hornet, but I should ignore him shooting me with his BB gun,
Dousing me with wallpaper glue. I try to rebuke his devil,
But he still pisses on my teddy Bear. Mom breaks a broom
Over his back for that. After he's washed, he's missing a nose.

3

People turn up missing in Mize, during the Watermelon Festival.
If you have the biggest melon, you may marry the watermelon queen
Cruising through town, on the hood of her convertible,
Waving at her fans. She's got great tits, her father a banker,
But you'll surely go to hell for gluttony, pride and ambition.
Such events are of the devil, the same lecherous devil that
Comes from lonely sinners who fornicate with dirty magazines.

4

I find pages partially burned in the barn, before helping
An uncle shuck corn. I see a breast, an eye and a guy's hairy ass.
The rest had been burned, the edges curled up.
I even find a Polaroid of three guys humping a watermelon.

5

"It's best to keep it in the sun all day so it's warm and juicy,"
My uncle says. When I ask him if it's a sin to do a watermelon,
He says, "The scriptures say we shouldn't waste the seed."
I ask if I can watch, and he says, "You betcha," and I can eat it
With him, afterwards, but I have to swallow the seeds.

Bildungsroman

The wind moves into the empty head and begins to give birth to its own little winds.

—"Seeds," Vasko Popa

I am someone I knew.
   Cotton-top head not beyond a ten-mile stretch of land

     And the pride of a preacher when I hide in the pulpit
      And sleep among the hymnals, the gospels that hold faith together.

But I am a trailer looking for a get-away hitch when my thimble
   Fills with prescribed desire and ain't nothing the church can do.

   Want lodges within me, I'm a sentence of confusion
     When one shoulder claims there's a turning point for God:

    If he forgives us all, what is left to forgive?
And the other—Denial is the truth of a body unable to walk.

Inevitably, briars refuse to settle along the fence line
   And make movement, joining my fields in holy matrimony.

2

Gigolo

My family fell apart, so I needed to get away.
How and by what means I didn't know,
So I stole from department stores,

Stuffing my bags with name-brand clothing.
Such balls I had, speaking to the clerk,
Asking for different sizes, only to buy socks.

I refunded those clothes to other stores
Until arrested. I wasn't always a hustler,
But I had to leave, so I learned to do whatever

To get by. It's not that bad in a rest area stall,
Being blown by an old guy, even if he's gumming.
With no teeth in the way, there's sure, pure sucking.

Grandma said that I'd go to hell for fornicating,
But it's hell being poor. Poverty may be the mother
Of instruction, but that education blows if stuck

In Raleigh, MS, a church bent on frightening sinners into heaven.
Plus, I wanted to see how far decent looks and my pathetic,
Vulnerable act got me. I surely succeeded, some life in New Orleans,

August heat, dancing on a bar, men fucking on the pool table,
Balls on balls in every corner. With *Oh Daddy, harder, Daddy,*
Fuck my hole, pop my brown cherry, it's hard to determine

Who wants a tea bagging, who wants to dry hump me,
Smell my ass, my boots to the brim with cash,
Beer bottles all across a sweaty, stinking bar,

My dick flapping from Viagra and stay-hard cream.
Near fainting, I was saved by an old man who sprayed me
With a water mister, which I gladly welcomed, for he took notice,

Said I reminded him of him when he was a young man
Needing a place to live, tired of sleeping on someone's couch.
He moved me into his guesthouse on Rue Dumaine,

Paying for all my meals while he told his life story,
His husband dying young, a motorcycle accident,
How he met him like he met me, only wanting to jack off.

Gosh, I said, is that all? I've been doing that since
That tall, pointing to a mutt on his hind legs:
I started on the lawnmower, the seat a bobbing,

So much vibration I cum, so good, I lost control,
Running over Grandpa's grave, blades bent to heaven and back.
I shot my load in every room, on the Lazy Susan, in the toilet,

In the tree house, in the shed, in the crevice of vinyl
Seats of a Ford Fairlane, in a Sunbeam bread bag,
A spoon handle up my ass. I didn't know his guesthouse

Was a set for shooting porn. Must be my big chance, I thought,
When offered 2,000 dollars to do a 30-minute segment.
I even picked out a name: Brick Bailey, hard as a brick,

Guaranteed a lay. But the shoot didn't go my way.
Who knew I was lactose intolerant?
Can happen anytime, anywhere, in one's life, my doctor said.

I felt like an overburdened cow, dehydrated, near death.
I heard Grandpa's voice, *Time to put him down.*
I moved out. *This porn is fuck fest, not shit fest,*

The director said, the old man too embarrassed for me
To hang around, so I joined Pamela, the one-armed prostitute
On Dauphine Street. That circus freak got all the action—

Men love cumming on her nub—so I got a gig at the Corner
Pocket known for pimply boys in stained underwear,
Dancing on the bar. I had blackheads but not pimples,

Both disgusting. But hey, if you're into that, man, so be it.
Who am I to pop the natural order of things?
I quit when Ms. Do, the owner, ends up dead, her throat

Slit, her Cadillac pushed into a bayou. That could be
Me, I thought, taking drugs that strangers
Give me, hoping that they'll be the one for me.

But she taught me something. When anyone asks,
What do you do? I respond, I don't do you.
Who am I kidding? I'll do anybody, fuck the cottage cheese

Of a fat lady, eat the ass of an old fart with dingle berries,
Fuck the armpit of a retard. I just need to get paid.
I could complain, but haven't I done enough?

But my life's good, by God. I can go anywhere,
Some how, as long as I'm needing and still willing.
I give them what they want, what I know to do.

Honky-Tonky Jail

I swear, I vow, I dare not drive again, I mean, drink-n-drive, again.
In jail, I'm cotton candy, musical chair for seventeen hard-ups.
No hymn, an elegy: no chance of bail, they don't care, they know the ropes,
So share. "If guilty, pour bleach on your hands, to keep keeping on," Keith says.
"In the can," Dan says, "Drain your dang-a-lang, Mister-Sister, Mister-Mam."
"Before a breath test, eat a PJ," BJ says, craving KFC.
I hand my PJ to Hess who says, "Better here than out there, homeless."
No bail, hell, so a Bailiff moves me to Population, on Lock-Down.
Not a routine trip—hairy hours on a bunk, on a bed I made.
"Look here, young buck, calm down," Tom says, "Or, I'll whip you in seven seconds."
Ray says, "Stay cool, Sonny boy. Shut your hole. Spread them legs. Show us your sun."
I quote Mr. T, LL Cool Jay, David Letterman, Chuck Norris,
My hole—a Cadillac converter, on cruise, passing all exit signs,
Until an intercom voice states my full name, the door sliding open.
Out, I take the short cut to the parking lot through high grass,
Morning dew spit-shining my shoes into twin suns, dime moments of I-told-you-so's.

Jail

God sends a friend to love me, but not the way I want it.
    "Maybe that's best," Mom says, "He's straight, a dog with problems."
I know—he can't forget his divorce, how he wants full custody

After she broke his nose when he said her pussy's like a wet paper bag.
    All of which is no wonder, she's a gold digger, and his life's hard, sister.
I can't help him. Only he can, but I doubt it. He feels sorry for himself,

Ruling his nest like a cock, pecking chicks out of line.
    I can listen, but Jesus, I have limits. If I hear one more
Goddamn word about his father's colostomy bag, his sister's

Single breast, his other sister on a breathing machine, in a coma,
    I may punch him. I'm not insensitive. I'm a hopeless romantic,
Lonely and sexually frustrated. O only if he loved me, perhaps

I'd put up with his bullshit. "Not ever and not today,"
    Mom says, "He don't deserve you, he'll fuck a jackass if somebody'd hold it still."
Now I have yet another issue, like making bail. Dad's the only landline number I know,

He comes through, but I must wait, he's in another state,
    And it's so freaking uncomfortable and unpleasant in a cell with seventeen guys.
I'm wearing Leon County underwear, for Mary's sake.

Lo, damnation, just when I finish counting from seven hundred backwards over and over,

      Nine hours in, my falling-asleep method, they move me to a stained leather chair

Facing a camera, a television broadcasting a court room, a judge dressed like an upright crow

With a You-fucked-up face. I'm asked if I'm who they think I am.

      I say, "Yes sir. I hope so, sir," and I'm pushed through a door where guys

Pace back and forth, holding their balls, proudly pushing them up,

Proudly letting them fall, bragging about what they done. I'm thinking, "It's do or get done."

      No chance of bail, they don't care. They know the ropes, and they share:

If you take a piss test, dip your hand in bleach. When in the bathroom, the officer watching,

Hold your dick and piss on your fingers, wiping all that junk right out.

      For a breath test: peanut butter. I offer my peanut butter sandwich to a crack head

Who keeps saying, "Better in here than out there, son."

I think that I'll be eating fried chicken real soon. I end up in general population,

      Dressed in scrubs, starving. Over my shoulder: a pillowcase with a towel,

Bar of soap, toothbrush, travel-sized toothpaste, and that's fucked up.

If I buy travel sizes, I'm taking a trip, one more charming and aromatic

      Than on the bunk I made myself. "Look here, young buck. Stay calm,"

The stranger below me says, "Or I'll whip your ass in fifteen minutes."

I don't ask, but did love drive him over the edge, to an ongoing storm?

Bond

I have one call, that's
All, so I call Dad who taught
Me to floor it, ditch

The law on a dirt
Road, but he's out of state, so
He says, "Hold on, son."

He calls my psychic
Who can't drive or pay cab fare.
Call Matt, I tell her.

"I'll take care of this,"
Dad says, calling my boyfriend.
"We all here?" Dad asks.

"Loud and clear," then Mom
Screaming, "What kind of psychic
Are you? You said my

Son would win millions,
Nothing about jail," so my
Psychic says, "Your son

Drank all day, left my
House after he overloaded
My washing machine."

I say, Excuse me.
I didn't drink all day. I
Took naps. "Let's all calm

Down," Dad says, "Listen
To me, Matt, in times like these,
We can't just turn to

Jesus, we have to
Turn to the yellow pages."
The first ad Matt turns

To is Emmanuel's
Bail Bonds, and Dad says, "Call him,
God's watching over my son."

Court

I'd rather pay an entrance fee to a puppet fight,

Place my bet on the ugly fat one. I could win enough money

To start over in sweet Alabama and open a sandal store

And sell cans of possum and gallons of Luzianne tea.

But there's no need to run. If it's not one thing,

It's another, so I roll with a circus show.

Besides, I got nowhere to go. Living on a stipend

Is tough, not enough to buy sirloin tips for Matt

Who tags along to chat me up. Thirty minutes early, we sit

On a lobby's pew where we learn that we both got saved at age six.

My dad drives a forklift, his dad makes school supplies.

But when the bailiff speaks, we follow him into the courtroom,

In a single line. He looks like Fat Albert,

But with a gun: Hey, Hey, Hey, O Hear ye, Hear ye.

Ice cream could uplift the men and women sitting on the left side

Of the room, in shackles, wearing scrubs, white socks

And white slippers greasy from sanitizing wash.

Give them leather masks, and this could be bondage porn,

One of a kind that I'd never buy or download.

Throw a licking llama in there, and we have a deal.

I'm reminded of when I was four and Doris had another devil in her.

Because I couldn't speak in tongues, they sent me

To the nursery where I had to say Jesus over and over

Or her devil would jump into me, and I wanted it.

I wasn't allowed to act like a fool in church.

I want it now. I can't stop starring at this unsightly woman

With sunken cheekbones. I fear she may get the "can" again

After she proudly admits to smoking crack on the way

To her friend's house. And what right did the officers have to arrest her?

Sure, she was driving, her license suspended, on the interstate,

But she kept her lawnmower on the side of the road,

Only crossed the median once, minding her own damn business.

She thought she saw her cousin's car pulled over, hazard lights on,

But it was some old lady in a tizzy, spanking her granddaughter

Kicking and screaming in the backseat, and what she gathered,

That girl deserved it. She could tell by her sassy look, she has a daughter

Just like that who won't take a whooping like a grownup.

Honestly, if this crack head keeps this life up, she won't live

Much longer, something the next guy knows something about.

While serving his thirty days from drinking a Colt 45

And driving on a suspended license, his newborn baby died.

He needs to make bail, or he'll lose his job, and he has three kids left to feed.

And his wife, well, she's not fit to work after losing her legs

In an accident with a drunk driver, and she had the smoothest legs around town,

So he's learned his lesson, he's giving up drinking, he's made arrangements

To get to work at the chicken plant, not the bus system, those routes

Aren't worth a dime in a quarter slot, "But don't you worry, your honor,

I'll make good on my promise," he says. Maybe the truth,

Maybe not, but sounds damn good, so good, he's released.

I should say I'm Mary when I drink, and I like her attitude.

She's a responsible polygamist who shares her Valtrex

Prescription, and because of her, your honor, I drink.

Would you like to have this woman in your head?

She won't shut up, and did I mention that she's bipolar?

She'll buy you a bottle of champagne, and before the night's over,

She'll throw a glass at you, she doesn't stop there, she'll punch you,

She'll throw a brick through your television, front door,

Whatever she can break, and she loves to lie, she likes

To cheat the system, the world owes her. She was neglected

As a child, as a human who dreamed of being a beauty queen,

She couldn't wear makeup, much less buy a dress

She couldn't wear to church. I'd be a fool to say this.

The judge may have a wife like her, well an ex-wife

Who got his house and Cadillac in a settlement, so I play it safe.

I want this to be over, now, not six long months of

Probation and community service, on a 12-Step program,

Pretending to give it to Jesus when Jesus has enough to deal with.

In the elevator, I ask Matt, How's our first date? "Definitely different," he says.

Probation

Ordered to do breath tests, I dial a number,
Listen to a recording, each morning, for six months.
If I hear Bailey, Bravo, or B as in Busted,

My ass struts to the big house where a guard
Shakes my hand on the way in, on the way out a scanner,
His middle finger joy-riding my palm,

A similar shake from an old man called Tater Head
Who hung out at the store across from my house,
Buying me jerky and spicy nuts, inviting me to his trailer

Any time I want. I decline his offer, I'm six, he's sixty,
I feel too welcomed, if you know what I'm saying,
But I groove with this receptionist slash breath-tester lady

Sporting acrylic pink nails with diamond tips.
She reminds me of my sister who tight-rolls her jeans,
Paints her face like Tammy Faye, mine too,

When I tag along on a secret date, too young to stay alone:
Mom's in the hospital, Dad's preaching at Sweet Water Church,
Two counties away, both of them unaware of us

Speeding down a dirt road in this sinner's truck
Nearly turning over after missing a cow, him shifting gears
Between my legs stinking of spilled beer,

His husky voice, "Dumb heifer liked to killed us,"
His cassette player blaring Def Leppard's "Love Bites."
If you play this tape backwards, you'll hear "Jesus,

Christ of Nazareth, can go to Hell."
Terrified, I want to go home, they want to screw,
Do the nasty, he wants up in her guts, so they

Drop me off at Grandma and Grandpa's, during a storm.
No one's home, the doors locked, the windows
Nailed shut, so I run to the barn where a mule's stomping a snake,

Not testing this snake's behavior, not waiting for venom
To prove itself. Out of breath, hungry, cold, and horny,
I take a disco nap in a hay loft, my hard-on jumping with thunder

Trotting on a tin roof, my dreams so big, my chest may burst,
Give in to hope, swelling. Half awake, I wonder, what if a mother ship
Dropped me off for a disturbing, reality t.v. show in rural Mississippi?

What if I'm a crossbreed in a fundamentalist experiment?
"What a riot," they say, watching the video feed,
"That fuckin' faggot is trying to speak in tongues,

Trying to prove himself to others that he's human."
What if the world has ended, the righteous on that escalator
To Jesus, and I didn't make the cut, didn't make it?

I can either prove my faith, die a martyr, or burn in a lake of fire, forever.
That was then, this is now: Feeling the vapors of my past,
This present, I say "Thanks" to the receptionist

Who says, "That will be five dollars," after I breathe into a tube,
Humming a certain octave. Proven sober, I walk home,
Weighing my actions, pissed off at the world, at myself,

Yet eager to prove myself to the powers-that-be stalking my spirit.
I've dealt with challenges far more grave, more eternal than this,
So why rest easy, now, why stop breathing, unraveling that noise within?

Goodwill

When I arrive at the back door, an old woman pricing shoes
With a sticker gun, pushing her bottom dentures in and out
With her tongue, says "Honey child, people die on that road."

And she's right. It's not safe bicycling on St. Augustine.
Cars with pagans pass me despite oncoming traffic,
Christians push me off the road. The manager, a bird-legged woman

Smoking Kools, asks, "How many hours you have, son?"
It's fifty for a D.U.I., so I'm told to dust the store.
I overhear customers complaining, "What a rip off, Velcro for a dollar?"

Another, "This Dover Edition's priced for a buck fifty."
"Yea, but it's Blake with an inscription, "To my heart sausage,"
I say, heading outside to beat the dust mop against a pole.

A woman, out of breath from inching her walker,
Grabs my arm, she points to an aquarium and asks,
"Is this a ten or twenty gallon?" "Neither," I say, "A fifty gallon

With a small crack, and not in a good way."
She tells me that I'm a smart man, I'd be smarter,
I'd look smarter, if I owned a stylish, ladder-style bookcase.

I ask the manager if she'd lower the price
From twenty to ten. She leans in, smacking grape gum,
And says, "You can have it, and you can leave early."

It's five minutes to closing, but hell yea, so I call a cab,
But this shelf's too long to fit in the trunk.
I'm not stupid—this bookshelf's practically new—

So I lock up the bike my neighbor lent me, determined
To walk home, moving this beauty from shoulder to shoulder,
Hoping to catch the bus nearby, but the bus doesn't come.

A church van passes me, one girl showing her breasts,
A boy showing his ant-bitten ass. Christ, what have I gotten myself into?
The church won't take me, but the devil will.

And then, Dear Masturbator, about a mile from home,
A man driving a red suburban, pulls over, he rolls down his window,
He says, "I've watched you carry that burden for miles."

Thirsty and worn out, I shoot the shit as he lowers his tailgate,
As he pops a mint, rubbing his crotch. It's a short drive
Between his stick shift and my legs, so he invites himself in,

But I say, "Oh no, you've done enough." Since I have stairs
To climb, why not? Once in, he doesn't want to leave, trying to befriend
My bird who goes for his diabetic, cholesterol eyes, my bird

Who rather die from the ceiling fan than be touched by him.
Birds know danger, they sense death, so I heed my bird's warning.
I say, "Look here," picking up a picture frame, tapping on that glass,

"Here's my boyfriend," a man with cracked teeth,
Tattoos of snakes and hookers birthing pigs, chainsaws,
Razors, and tampons, a mug-shot of a rapist that I printed

And framed for a moment like this, when a stranger's intention
And goodwill is called into question. "He looks like a killer,"
He says. "Could be," I say, "He's known for a beer in one hand

And a bat in the other." Opening my closet door, I say, "Here's his bat,"
And "Oh, he's here now," when my neighbor pulls into the driveway,
This man good as gone, slamming the door off its hinges.

Greyhound

I find my boyfriend, not in the future tense, but the one
I'm dating on a porn site, asking for private photos,
Poppers and bondage sex, so I jump the gray dog to visit

Mama who's sure to console me with her casseroles
And cakes, plus I'm a sucker for discipline and told-you-so's,
Whatever it takes for me to write these experiences

Up firsthand. I wish I were on that bus that overturned
On an exit ramp and slid into a field, killing three cows,
A deadbeat father and a penniless addict. According

To a survivor in a chat room, one paramedic,
Remarking about the fast-food wrappers and lottery
Tickets, said, "Chicken nuggets and gambling's a bad

Combination." But now, my fellow thrill-seeker, look at
This guy who's wearing a cap with bold letters, "My inner
Child needs a spanking." I wonder if he reads Wordsworth,

But before I ask, I'm interrupted. "Don't talk to him,"
The Goth girl next to me in platform boots, whispers,
"I know you just got on, like, and I don't want to scare you,

Like, but I've been on this bus all night, like, and it's like,
Ahhh, like a mother-fucking, like, end-of-time movie.
And Roberta, like, behind us, like, is on her way to see

Her aunt who believes we're already, like, dead." I turn around,
Expecting to see a woman bearing henna tattoos and sitting
In the lotus position, but she's pulling a french fry

From between her gorilla titties and humming "Wild Thing."
But she's not as gassy as the horse-faced man in front of us,
Quoting Cheech and Chong as if they're a part of God's plan.

When I thought he couldn't go on, he stands up and screams,
"I'm a paramedic," after a woman with untidy, gray-streaked
Hair collapses in the aisle, her hand clutching a photo

Of a man wearing overalls and holding a Shih Tzu over
A birthday cake. It's clear that he doesn't have any training.
Not the dog, but this man saying, "Work with me, work with me."

I'm reminded of a church service when Brother Roy Ulmer
Faints in the spirit, shits too, during a testimony. My cousin
Sybil, a real paramedic, and the only one to go to college

In my church, well, my entire family, says, "This ain't good.
He ain't breathing." If you look up death and excretion,
And you get a page error, you need faster cable or you

Have to reset your browser. Apparently, Brother Roy
Ulmer has a good connection. After God jumps into Sybil
And tells her to do what she's been trained to do—perform

CPR—he comes back to life only to live one week longer,
Enough time to finish refurbishing the pine pews with velvet,
And to tell his daughter that she isn't his daughter.

Luckily, we're a few miles from the Mobile terminal.
While watching this lady's body carried off the bus, I smoke a cigarette.
A man walks up to me, shakes his head, and says, "What a shame."

Surely is, but he's not talking about this lady: he's complaining
About the chicken basket he bought in the station deli.
"Shit, look at her," he says, holding up a potato log, "Ain't this

The most droopiest thang you ever saw?" "Well," I say, "I suppose
You don't know Ronny," but before I finish, we're told to board.
An army cadet sits next to me, and says, "Hell, it's about to be

Nuts to butts up in here." "Sounds terrible," I say, "What's your name?"
He's Sam from Arkansas, and he believes in destiny,
But also the choice to fuck it up. He tells me a bedtime story:

While watching Thriller at his friend's house, his friend told his dad
To pour his own whiskey, so his dad pulled down his friend's pants
And whipped his hairy butt with a clothes hanger.

I'm shameful, I think, for beating my ex-boyfriend like a dog,
And telling him that I could care less if he died, but I'm devastated
After he throws himself in front of an eighteen-wheeler.

Years later, Sam visited that old man being fed through a tube.
"You're making the right choice," Sam says, patting my shoulder,
When I throw my cigarettes out the window, my only friends who don't talk back.

3

Death

Able to lose three pints of blood

        Before room temperature,

  Rolling over yonder,

           Taking a dirt nap, pushing up the daisies,

      Passing over, on, away,

    Stiff & stoned to meet our maker,

We began with a cell

       Now a multitude of cells,

   A species shuffling off our mortal coil,

        Joining the choir invisible

     On that good night of a better place

   Beyond the promised shore,

67

That bar of River Styx in Elysian Fields,

Paying Charon's fare,

Sleeping with the fishes,

We began with a tooth,

Little sparrow-bone,

Cut off, defunct, done for,

Erased, extinct, inanimate, gone,

Late, liquidated & mortified,

Offed, perishing in repose,

Rubbed out, snuffed out, wasted,

Bumping off, cashing in,

Cashing out, dancing our last dance,

Eating it, taking it like a man,

Crouching toward Bethlehem

On a one-way ticket

From where

We began

On the back of a Greyhound

Returned to sender,

Adios Park, Corpses-R-Us,

La Chateau Eternity,

Hearse-Pit Stop

In the city of Necropolis

Known for farewells and hellos,

Minutes of flame with a one-person chamber

Where the moon shineth not,

A free feel for all

Who dig a done-for-deadbeat,

A clammy Sonata for 1,

A sticky end.

Nightshift

In memory of Jason McBride

Awake yet asleep
a state of paralysis
I can't move or speak

haunted
by tall
lanky
black-human forms

lurking
around my bed
a tramping ground

their eyes
like roaring lions
that walk about

ready

to devour

*

is this

what it feels like

to be dead

and not wanting death

I've heard

that when we die

we don't know

until told otherwise

*

this time

I see him

so I rise

from my body

I take his hand

If I could speak

I'd tell him
if the ground shook
opened up
swallowed us all
I'd willingly go
so long as
he's by my side

If I could speak

I'd tell him
how life is
without him

a pear
in the sand

oil drums

in my bones

a bar

lacking their Karaoke King

I want to wake

but the night's

not done

so we take a drive

on a dirt road

listening to thunder

caught in the clouds

then on a train that explodes

I tell him Goodbye

but he's not ready to go

no not yet

he opens my bedroom door
and a black cat

that I befriended
knocks over the candle
burning for him

I wake
stunned by his presence
his whiskey breath
confused by what he whispers
Biggest train disaster

*

Why did he walk
drunk
across the interstate

why did he
choose

that speeding eighteen-wheeler
did he stumble

did his glasses
fall off

*

He doesn't answer
these questions
but I'm in Mississippi
and a bomb
explodes in Spain

My Predecessors

Used to frighten me in the night

Broken, fulfilled songs

Dimensions

Boldface obituaries

Demanding me to read their books,

Perhaps their poems

An antenna to the past,

A socket and key

To my future,

Their bodies rinsed of the carnal,

The preoccupation of flesh and bones,

Their spirits, well, I can only assume,

Desire my abstractions—

My hopes, my fears, my truths.

I am their concentration, a spell.

Their names
I shall not list them all,

But what do they want?

What absolution
May I impart?

I too am a guest
In my home,

A fire in a hull,
In search of meaning,

So I offer my friendship,

"You're all welcome to stay,
But you must help with the rent," I say,
"And wash the fucking dishes, bitches."

                I imagine them saying that they
        Take their eggs over easy, or else,

As they fade
        Into the morning flow,
                Eager to eat the world
        One scare at a time

Until finding a state of grace,
        Or whatever they're looking for.

The Tree Frog, The Owl, The Bumblebee

The ducks return to Chapman Pond today.
I have a trial run for the Cornish hens
Stuffed with garlic, pearl onions, potatoes.
The hens come out singing, "I'll Fly Away."
The potatoes weren't done, but still juicy.

The tree frog leaps to dinner, joins the song,
Then takes a nap on my oriental plate.
The owl comes too, hooting so joyfully,
Then silently, so swiftly swoops away.

We finish the hens deliciously done.
For dessert—Elvis's "Polk Salad Annie,"
The bumblebee's hum around the deck table.

A glass ashtray jumps off the railing,
Lands beneath the stairwell, still in one piece.
I feel, we feel, a common bond with life,
Linked to the mysterious, unseen world.

My guests go home, I'm glad to be alone.

Do I Dare Disturb the Universe?

Wee-wee-sweet-pea me?
      I live, I weep, a third of me
passed in sleep,
          start a scene or two,
     play and dance the fool,
          roll back the curtain for the muse.

I live for depth, less so a lengthy life,
         nor deny the natural order of things,
     but must I be swept so soon
          to the sweet by and by?

     Life's always so, so pleasing,
so why should death be so displeasing?

     O Death, so kind, so cruel, graciously unfair,
         such a trump card, such a trollop, common denominator,
          master and servant to class.

O Life, to live, to be a rare steak less traveled by.
     Why just exist?
   That's not it at all, not at all—
         to the point of tears,

get-up-and-go, oomph, brio, orbit, yo-yo,
strut,   fret,   fetch,
keep the wolf from the door,
scratch where it itches,
pull some nothing from thin air,
rush, stir, trip, wear and tear.

I walk upon the earth, spared another day,
another hour upon the stage.

A motor with a plan,
I am man,

homo, member, party,
I bust a nut, kick, yield, recording my days,
intent, tone, heart, spirit,
a life sentence,
no shame, no game,

I question, seek, shall not always find,
I backup on a dead-end road,
look up, look down upon,
sympathize with an ant
carrying a wing over mountainous mud, dirt, scum.

I waste time, murder, create, anticipate,
                stub my toe
      where I come and go, O, O, O, O,

O,   Sticky-Sweet Peach,
            come home, pull up a chair,
                  cast a spell on my chinny-chin chin.

I rather be cross-eyed—
         one eye that says shit to the other—
            than not see at all,

 cut out my tongue if not cheeky

   if I'm to be a ragged claw,
         cantankerous, impermeable membrane,
            a closed field with shards of glass among blades of grass.
   I rather be be-headed, served on a platter,
if denied a full head of hair,
      fingers run through my hair.

O,   Open Field,
             measureless,   perpetual uncertainty,

dance with me under the honky moonlight,

in broad daylight,

do me roughly half a day but all night long,

in the quickening of the night,

the quiet, quite-loud night,

owls echoing dactyls and spondees,

thrashers tweeting thank-you's.

Bump me, I bump back,

atqui vivere, militare est,

la petite mort, each day, s'il vous plait.

I will not end it all on a railroad,

take a colossal heroin-hit,

kneel on grits,

slip on soap,

eat poisonous, cherry pie.

Amen,   thunderous whisper.

4

He Found a Diamond, a Big-Ass Diamond

He found a diamond, an uncut diamond
    Worth millions, the answer to his problems.

"Well," he thought, "I shouldn't get carried away,"
    So he got carried away. He charted a helicopter,

He leased a limousine, he rescued his mother
    From the daycare, his father from the forklift,

He bought his grandma's dentures, his sister
    A double-wide trailer, paid his brother's

Child support, he replaced his aunt's hips,
    He took a flight to space, lived on Park Place,

He built homeless shelters, he took a cruise,
    He ate bison, ate python, drank tiger's blood,

He got his teeth fixed, he got a face-lift,
    He took advantage of Gay for Pay, loved

Getting something extra for little cost,

      He bought valets for vowels, he courted

Consonants, he pimped-out prepositions,

      He conceived conjunctions, pardoned fragments,

He wasted water, made his mark on a beach,

      "This is all mine, mine, this is all mine, mine,"

Then he watched all his dreams wash away

      When he heard, "It's windshield glass," the jeweler

In the mall says, "Worthless windshield glass,

      Ain't worth nothing, nada, not even my time."

"Shit, Look At Her," he says, Holding Up a Potato Log

At the Greyhound Terminal in Mobile,
        Alabama, I smoke a cigarette

While watching a dead lady carried off
        The bus. A man walks up to me, shaking

His head, and says, "What a shame."
        Surely is, but he's not talking about this lady.

He's complaining about the chicken basket
        He bought in the station deli.

"Shit, look at her," he says, holding up a potato log,
        "Ain't this the most droopiest thang

You ever saw?" Well, I say, I suppose you
        Don't know Ronny, and you're better off.

He works at a mental hospital, plays his guitar,
        The only song he knows, with his teeth.

At my birthday party, before friends arrive,
        He gives me a book on correct grammar,

And I'm an English major, then he says,
   "Hey man, I've got crabs, and you probably

Got crabs too." Woe is I: I'm a hairy guy,
   Buying a kit of poison with a tiny comb.

This man, still holding up the potato log,
   Looks at me, looks at his potato log,

Then says, "Man, you've been straight
   With me, that's cool, but I'll never eat

A potato log again, and that hurts, Bro,"
   Throwing his chicken basket to the curb.

We Must Save Ourselves

Be not forgetful to entertain strangers:
some have entertained angels unawares.

I'm looking for my savior on subways,
Is he this man pushing half himself
On a skate board, from car to car,
Singing I have no legs, I have no legs,

I'm looking for my savior in coffee shops
Of contemplation and sober hook-ups,
I'm reading the Tao de Ching,
Well, I'm reading the Tao of Pooh,

I'm looking for my savior in the waiting room
Of my psychiatrist, is he this autistic child
Chastising a middle-aged woman,
Gosh, you're fat, really fat, do you know that,

I'm looking for my savior in the checkout line,
Is he this screaming toddler in a buggy,
Slapped, spanked then consoled with sugar,
This wife back-talking her deadbeat husband,

Shit! You a damn lie, yo black ass b keeping d kids tonight,
I'm looking for my savior outside liquor stores,
Is he this man soliciting pity for a fix,
Bro, can you help a bro out, my back tire's flat,

I'm looking for my savior in the country,
Is he that suicidal heifer in the middle of the dirt road,
Chewing cud like no man's business,
I'm looking for my savior in two lanes, three lanes,

Four lanes, five lanes, six lanes, seven lanes, O holler,
Is he this guy driving a Mini-Cooper
With a gun-rack, deer horns on the hood,
His bumper sticker Gay for Pay, Whatever Way,

I'm looking for my savior among night terrors
And nocturnal emissions, during awkward,
Intolerable moments, like when I invite a friend
Of a friend to a friend's party, and he

Gets smashed, talks about his problems all night,
Then indignant when called out on his behavior,
An awkward moment, indeed, when I realize,
The next day, that I was that asshole,

That self-appointed Eeyore of the evening,
I'm looking for my savior in office buildings,
Is he this night janitor polishing the floors,
Singing It's a Mean Old World to live in,

I'm looking for my savior from within,
Is he that grey matter buried in grooves,
Is he what's happening in the hypothalamus,
Is he that voice promising to make it all better,

That drum stirring the living from their sleep,
That calm & final knock on the door,
Is my savior out there, here in this crowd,
If so, stand, introduce yourself, be proud

To pay my tab, to pay my rent, pay off
My student loans, buy me a home, a home
In my name, paid for, paid in full, not just
Any home, one that I can call my own.

The Cake Rising

Thank you, Koch

How embarrassing when the cake, fresh out the oven, breaks apart.
Only a sincere host can understand the seriousness of this moment.
A failed cake will not go unnoticed, unless some libation occurs.

To boil water is easy, not serious at all, but a fucked-up cake,
Well, the host should serve it as is, accept the ridicule of guests,
Or improvise. Blend that batter, pack it tightly in ramekins,

Pour icing on that disaster, and hope for the best.
I recommend that you serve it late in the evening,
After wine, whiskey & stinky weed, then they'll praise you.

O, seriousness, why are you so serious?
I can talk to the cake all I want, but a cake isn't a plant,
A cake isn't a bird, a cake isn't a hurricane.

To bake a cake isn't as easy as one may think,
Surely if one's incapable of following directions.
To bake a cake must be a serious event if you're an anarchist.

To die is easy. To be born is an uneasy affair.
To be hit by an acorn, well, that's not serious at all,
Unless you're an ant, a mosquito, an insect, etc.

To take an upper and a downer could be serious.
Losing wisdom teeth to make room for wisdom,
And one is just as dumb when they arrive, is serious.

If the only warmth in one's home is a toaster oven,
And still expecting a pre-approved credit card, well,
That's not necessarily serious, that's just stupid.

A serious moment for the fly is when it's fly-swatted to death.
A serious moment for a duck is when there's no pond to land in.
Yes, our life is serious, some lives more serious than others.

To face our fear is serious. To suffer to create is serious.
To feel so good to be missed by someone is serious.
Having no soul to save is serious for a priest.

The fact that this poem has an audience issue isn't that serious.
If this were a presidential speech, this would be serious.
The seriousness of this poem are the glimpses

Of our mortality among the trivial and the mundane.

A serious moment for this poem is when deciding to end it.

A poem like this can go on and on.

THE END

Scott Bailey grew up in Raleigh, Mississippi, the former home of the National Tobacco Spitting Contest. He comes from a family of preachers and carpenters. Although he spoke in tongues, on the women's side of the altar, at Crossroads Holiness Church, he never learned how to pound a nail. His degrees include a B.A. in English, Summa Cum Laude, an M.A. in Creative Writing from the College of Arts & Letters, The University of Southern Mississippi, an M.F.A. in Creative Writing from New York University, and a Ph.D. in English from Florida State University. He has received fellowships from Florida State University, The Mississippi Arts Commission, New York University, and The Valparaiso Foundation in Spain.

9 781630 450021